Darcey Bussell

Darcey Bussell

hardie grant books
MELBOURNE · LONDON

LORD SNOWDON 1991

It was always exciting to do a poster for a new work. Our costumes were not ready for the new production of *Winter Dreams*, so Lord Snowdon had the idea of photographing us naked! This came as a slight shock as we didn't know this when we arrived at the shoot. *Winter Dreams* is based on Chekov's *Three Sisters* and in this photo I am with Niccy Tranah and Viviana Durante.

Foreword

During my first years as Director of The Royal Ballet, Sir Peter Wright, at that time Director of Sadler's Wells Royal Ballet (now Birmingham Royal Ballet) and I would meet annually to discuss the merits of the graduating students of The Royal Ballet School and decide between us which of them would join which company. Some of these meetings became amicable battles for, if the class had in its midst a student with exceptional gifts and talent, our eyes would inevitably alight on that same person. This situation was no more evident than in 1987 when the graduate in question was Darcey Bussell. Sir Peter pleaded his case well; he was looking to the near future and needed a dancer who would bypass the *corps de ballet* and rapidly take on soloist and principal roles to become a new home-grown ballerina. I gave in to his pleas and he consoled me by saying that one day, this beautiful and talented young woman might wish to stretch her wings in new territory on the Opera House stage – little did we know, at that moment, how soon that was to be.

The Royal Ballet's founder, Dame Ninette de Valois, held the strong belief that choreographers were the lifeblood of a ballet company. To us as dancers they were the stars and throughout my career, both as a dancer and eventually as Director, I was incredibly fortunate to work with two of the greatest creative forces of The Royal Ballet, Sir Frederick Ashton and Sir Kenneth MacMillan.

It was Kenneth who would radically alter the path that Darcey's career would take. In the eighties he had spent time with the American Ballet Theatre in New York where he enjoyed the 'climate change' of working with a different company, and was inspired and excited by the more athletic style and competitive spirit that seems inherent in the American dancer. In 1988, he embarked on a major reworking of Benjamin Britten's ballet score *The Prince of the Pagodas* for The Royal Ballet and was looking for a young dancer to create the ballet's heroine, Princess Rose. With images of the American dancers still in the forefront of his mind, he needed someone who was not only young and beautiful but also, a dancer of great technical and physical strength. He found his muse in Sadler's Wells Royal Ballet – Peter had lost his 'battle' and Darcey transferred to The Royal Ballet.

The role of Princess Rose became a tour de force for Darcey. Kenneth stretched her talent and stamina to the limits and she rose to every challenge magnificently. Here, suddenly, was a new and exciting star in the making and I was thrilled that she was emerging 'under my wing'. After one of her glorious performances in *Pagodas* it gave me enormous pleasure and pride to promote her to the ranks of Principal Dancer.

What followed was her progression into the roles of the great 19th century classical ballets, The Royal Ballet's own heritage repertory and many new creations. Very soon, she began to attract a critical and public interest that grew rapidly, taking her beyond Covent Garden into the wider realms of the media. Fashion shoots, public appearances, car promotions, physical fitness publications, dancewear ranges were some of the things that came her way but happily, despite every additional request and pressure, and the extra time and energy these activities demanded, she remained completely committed to and focused on her daily rehearsal and performance schedule.

It is possible that, to any young dance student, it might appear that Darcey's meteoric rise to stardom and the successes and benefits that accompanied it, were without obstacle or disappointment. This was certainly not the case and she endured any problems or setbacks that arose along the way with the stoicism and professionalism that are so much a part of her personality.

As I look back, I realise how fortunate I was to have had in The Royal Ballet during my time as Director, a ballerina who gave me so much pride and pleasure as I watched her become a star of the ballet world and also a glamorous celebrity in her own right; a star whose light always reflected back on the company to which she was so loyal. My treasured dance memory of her is of a performance when I was appearing as Carabosse in my own production of *The Sleeping Beauty*. I watched Darcey from the wings effortlessly sail through the exacting demands of Princess Aurora's first entrance, the Rose Adage and her solo variation. As a dancer, I knew only too well the hours of preparation and frustration that had gone in to that performance; all the anxieties and pitfalls that beset a performer as they prepare for a major role. But that evening, for me, all Darcey's glorious qualities of elegance, glamour, power and purity of technique shone out. The role was hers and hers alone.

These days, Darcey and I have both moved on from life in The Royal Ballet but one never really loses the family ties that The Royal Ballet, wonderful company that it is, creates. Now, our paths cross only occasionally but in these brief meetings the Darcey 'glow' radiates as strongly as ever and as we part, I feel the better for it.

Sir Anthony Dowell CBE
Former Principal Dancer and Director of The Royal Ballet

London, June 2012

ANNIE LEIBOVITZ OCTOBER 1991

I went to New York after a Royal Ballet tour in Orange County, California. I had two days on my own being shot for *Vanity Fair* on Annie's roof. I was put in outfits ranging from giant angel feathered wings which were very heavy, to gold lamé bodices. At one point the backdrop set fell down on me as it was a windy day. I remember Annie shouting 'get it off her!' to her six male assistants. Finally we ended up in Annie's studio and I got to wear a beautiful red dress (opposite).

KODAK PXP 6057

JILLIAN EDELSTEIN MAY 1993

Jillian took this cool photograph for *The Daily Telegraph*. Jonny and I arrived at a tiny studio in our practice clothes, having come straight from rehearsal. All I did was slip on my practice tutu, then we hit a couple of poses and we were done in no time at all. I call this shot 'Jonathan as my rock'.

Introduction

When I think back on my 20-year career as a dancer, I cannot imagine having done anything else. I started at The Royal Ballet School at age 13 and in my first year I was told by a teacher that this was not for me and that I should give up if I couldn't take all the corrections. Luckily I was so stubborn and wanted to prove her wrong. I was determined to make the most of this opportunity. After graduating at age 17, I was offered a job with Sadler's Wells Royal Ballet in the corps de ballet, under the direction of Sir Peter Wright. I was told that as it was a smaller Company, I would get some solo work. I performed many solo roles and one Principal role in *Elite Syncopations* at aged 18. I didn't appreciate at the time how much more experience I gained in my first year at Sadler's Wells. If I had joined The Royal Ballet, a much larger and structured Company, I wouldn't have been given those same roles. I loved Sadler's Wells but after only one year there, my life changed. It was decided that I would move to the resident Company, The Royal Ballet, to be a soloist. The brilliant choreographer Sir Kenneth MacMillan was looking for a young talent to dance the role of Princess Rose in his new ballet *The Prince of the Pagodas*. In the first year, I had to start learning a whole new repertoire, whilst at the same time working with Sir Kenneth MacMillan and Jonathan Cope on the new work. In December 1989, at the start of only my second year at The Royal Ballet, we opened *The Prince of the Pagodas* and at the end of the first show, while still on stage, I was promoted to Principal. I was aged 20. The next few years was when I really learnt my trade, experiencing for the first time The Royal Ballet's rich classical repertoire including *Swan Lake*, *La Bayadère* and *The Sleeping Beauty*. In these technically exacting ballets I had to learn to pace myself and explore the subtleties of the role within their structured form.

I found my job was my passion, and I had an automatic drive in me to keep striving for perfection. I tried to learn from all the mistakes I made and incorporate my life experiences as I went along. What is not always apparent are the disappointments that occur over a long dance career. I twice incurred injuries just before the first nights of a new Season and I had two operations on my right ankle. Early in my career I was famously miscast with Irek Mukhamedov for *Manon* and I was removed only two weeks before the first night. There were these low moments, but I pretended there were very few of them, and just got on with it. Even with the discipline, the repetition, the hard work and the emotional ups and downs of any dancer's life, I knew I was the most fortunate person.

An important part of a dancer's career is to have works created on you. What I loved was working intimately with choreographers and creating something new. It was such a rewarding process to be an integral part of the history of the work. However intense the rehearsals became I knew how privileged I was to work with people like Sir Kenneth in *Winter Dreams*, Christopher Wheeldon in *Pavane* and John Neumeier in *Lento*.

I never wanted to be typecast as one style of dancer, and I was determined to surprise people and show that I had versatility, even though I was a tall dancer for my time. I particularly enjoyed George Balanchine's style with its pure lines and physical attack. Works such as *Apollo* were so far ahead of their time and I never tired of trying to perfect their seamless lines. I enjoyed dancing Balanchine's work so much so that I once seriously considered an offer to leave London to work at the New York City Ballet. In the end I did not choose that path but I never lost my love of all things Balanchine.

I was very privileged to guest with many other famous ballet companies including having the rare opportunities to dance with the Kirov and La Scala, which came about because of my famous international partners, Igor Zelensky and Roberto Bolle. Experiencing different theatres, repertoires and partners was very exciting, but it was always the kindness and comraderie of the Company members that made those times so memorable.

Above all, I was so lucky to have had nearly 20 years with The Royal Ballet working with my two Directors Sir Anthony Dowell and Dame Monica Mason. My final performance at the Royal Opera house on 8th June 2007 was *Song of the Earth*, choreographed by Sir Kenneth MacMillan. I first performed this ballet in 1990 and it made a deep and lasting impression on me. Given that Sir Kenneth had been so instrumental at the start of my career, this was a very special and poignant end to my time at The Royal Ballet.

Early in my career I made a conscious decision to work with professional photographers who asked to photograph me dancing, in the studio, on stage or on a photographic shoot. I knew these were great opportunities to work with such talent and I loved the creative process. I cannot say how extraordinary it has been to work closely with so many renowned photographers. They all wanted to achieve the same standards in their art form that I strived for in my dancing. A studio photo shoot was sometimes harder than a performance for me. These shoots normally took about four hours, required extraordinary patience and weren't fluid, so my muscles would often get cold in the process.

After finishing my dancing career, I realised I had so much material and I didn't want to forget anything. I wanted this book to show my respect for everyone involved in dance and capture the passion of this wonderful art. And, of course, having two girls of my own, I also wanted them to remember their mother as a dancer.

It was never going to be a conventional working life and I wouldn't have had it any other way.

Darcey

1

The Early Years

Taken while my mother was on a photo shoot in Kensington Gardens, London. She was a popular clothes designer on the Kings Road in the early 1970s. I am aged one and had been running since the age of 10 months. My mother has clearly been able to stop me moving for a second for this photo to be taken. I don't think anyone would have thought that these legs were going to be a dancer's.

Autumn Leaves
1984
THE ROYAL BALLET UPPER SCHOOL,
WHITE LODGE, LONDON

I remember this as being the first time I was really noticed whilst in my last year at White Lodge, aged 15. A fellow pupil, Michael Rolnick, created a lovely, slow and lyrical piece that belied his age, for the school's choreographic evening. Despite being White Lodgers, we were asked to perform it at The Royal Ballet Upper School, which is unheard of. I was amazed that some of the eighteen year old students complimented me on the quality of my dancing.

Concerto

JULY, 1986

THE ROYAL BALLET SCHOOL, ROYAL OPERA HOUSE,
COVENT GARDEN, LONDON

My first school performance was the solo role
from the 3rd movement, when I had just turned
17. I suffered the great disappointment of having
to half-mark my rehearsal when the great Sir
Kenneth MacMillan came to watch. I had over-
strained my hamstring from pushing the jumps
too hard. I desperately wanted to prove to him
that I was the right dancer for the role and
fortunately for me, he did get to see the finished
product in the school performance. This was my
first solo on the Royal Opera House stage and
while dancing this I remember hyperventilating,
due to a mixture of the stamina required and my
nerves. This role led to Kenneth choosing me for
The Prince of the Pagodas two years later.

Swan Lake

JULY, 1987

THE ROYAL BALLET SCHOOL, ROYAL OPERA HOUSE,
COVENT GARDEN, LONDON

My last School Performance was in my graduating
year of 1987. Rachael Whitbread and myself were
both offered places on the Australian tour with
The Royal Ballet Company, for experience as
students. We chose to stay and perform Act 3 of
Swan Lake as we both felt it was better to be able
to prove yourself in such an important Principal
role at this age. It was exciting to perform the
seductive role of Odile with Stuart Cassidy, my
fellow pupil. After the school performances
finished, I was offered a contract by Sir Peter
Wright to join Sadler's Wells Royal Ballet.

Darcey and I spent a year with Sadler's Wells performing and touring from Sunderland to Tokyo. What was amazing at that time was the sheer physicality and energy of Darcey's dancing... Like nothing we had seen before...

KEVIN O'HARE (DIRECTOR, THE ROYAL BALLET COMPANY)

La Bayadère
MAY, 1989
JIMMY WORMSER'S STUDIO, LONDON

One of my first posters for The Royal Ballet, this is in fact not a step from Gamzatti's repertoire. This didn't matter to Jimmy Wormser, an exuberant and inspiring photographer who shot a lot of posters for The Royal Ballet. He wanted me to try as many spectacular jumps as possible and using a trampoline was his trick of not tiring out the dancers he was photographing. Jimmy was a dear friend with such personality and an infectious laugh that it was impossible not to enjoy yourself when you were working with him.

La Bayadère

MAY, 1989

THE ROYAL BALLET, COVENT GARDEN, LONDON

My first Principal role, Gamzatti, came when I was still a Soloist at The Royal Ballet. I had only been in the Company for about six months. This was Natasha Makarova's production and she rehearsed me ruthlessly, which was understandable. I got to perform with the Principal dancer Jonathan Cope and fortunately for me, he was very encouraging and gave me great confidence. Nevertheless, with my lack of experience, I used to pester him to work on all my turns and hitting all the balances in the 15 minutes before the curtain was due to go up. He would just say 'Look, we have done enough rehearsals, you know what to do'.

Galanteries

APRIL, 1990

THE ROYAL BALLET, COVENT GARDEN, LONDON

A beautiful one-act work by David Bintley which I felt very priviledged to perform. At this stage of my career this was a technically very difficult *pas de deux* for me, as I had little experience of modern ballet. Fortunately it was very lyrical and suited my length and reach. Jonathan manoeuvred me perfectly. He wisely advised me to concentrate on creating great lines, while he did the rest. I had obviously forgotten one of the corrections from my first Director Sir Peter Wright, which was to keep my mouth closed when I danced.

Song of the Earth

MAY, 1990
THE ROYAL BALLET, COVENT GARDEN, LONDON

Choreographed by Sir Kenneth MacMillan, *Song* made a deep and lasting impression on me. I was very fortunate to be able to perform such a meaningful work at the age of 21. The experience and quality of my partners, Antony Dowson and Bruce Sansom, gave me the freedom and confidence to explore this extraordinary role. The only other time I performed this ballet was for my very last show with the Company, seventeen years later.

Elite Syncopations

OCTOBER, 1990

THE ROYAL BALLET, COVENT GARDEN, LONDON

This was my first Principal role in Sadler's Wells Royal Ballet in 1988. I was blissfully unaware of the importance of the role I had been given and I even missed my first rehearsal as I thought I was one of the solo girls and not the Principal girl. Choreographed by Sir Kenneth MacMillan, this ballet is incredibly cool and sophisticated and set to Joplin's ragtime music. I loved this role from the moment I started rehearsals. My first performance of *Elite* with The Royal Ballet was soon after, in October 1990, when this photo was taken.

Agon

APRIL, 1991

THE ROYAL BALLET, COVENT GARDEN, LONDON

It was the *pas de deux* in *Agon* that started
my love affair with George Balanchine's
choreography. The abstract moves and
physical attack of *Agon* suited my physicality.
Choreographed in 1957 and created on a black
and white couple, the man and the woman try
to assert dominance over each other. During
this Season I got to perform with both Chris
Saunders, and Guest Artist Eddie Shellman from
Dance Theatre of Harlem.

The Sleeping Beauty

JANUARY, 1993

THE ROYAL BALLET, COVENT GARDEN, LONDON

———

The famous Rose Adage is only perfected with experience. In my first performances as Aurora, I thought I could smile at my four princes and the audience during the renowned balances. I slowly realised I had to spot on the floor or on the costume of my partner to achieve the musical spectacle, and then I was able to enjoy taking the risks which make the Rose Adage very exciting to watch. Pictured here with Adam Cooper, as one of my main four Princes.

The Sleeping Beauty

JANUARY, 1993

The Sleeping Beauty

JANUARY, 1993

THE ROYAL BALLET, COVENT GARDEN, LONDON

With our matching classical styles, Jonathan Cope and I were able to create clarity within the celebrated Act 3 of *The Sleeping Beauty*. Jonny was an extraordinary partner and he gave me the confidence necessary for us to be natural together within the classics. This meant that I felt like a real person on stage instead of just acting out the fairytale Princess.

2

First Classics

Swan Lake

OCTOBER, 2000

THE ROYAL BALLET, COVENT GARDEN, LONDON

I call this my first official classic. Even though I had experienced The *Prince of the Pagodas*, *Swan Lake* was very challenging at the age of 20, as I was still learning how to sustain my technique for three and a half hours. These rehearsal photos are taken later in my career with Roberto Bolle, my partner for the last seven years of my career. He is a beautiful dancer and a superb partner, and he never got tired of rehearsing day in and day out with me. Even with all the experience of many performances, we would still do three to four weeks of rehearsals before the first show of the Season. I needed this time due to the technique and stamina required to play the two roles. When the ballet originated in the 19th century, Odette and Odile were played by two ballerinas.

Swan Lake

OCTOBER, 2000

THE ROYAL BALLET, COVENT GARDEN, LONDON

Performing in Sir Anthony Dowell's elaborate production of Petipa's and Ivanov's masterpiece. Here, Rothbart the sorcerer is played by the wonderful Christopher Saunders. He is using his powers to control me in the very dramatic last bourrées of Act 2. In the opposite image I'm in a very distinctive penché of the famous Act 2 *pas de deux*, both the slight bend of the leg and the broken wrist are resembling the wings of a swan.

Swan Lake

OCTOBER, 2000

THE ROYAL BALLET, COVENT GARDEN, LONDON

In one of the beautiful moves from the second
act *pas de deux*, Roberto brings me out of this
deep arch incredibly smoothly into a deep
penché. I got to perform *Swan Lake* in many
countries around the world, but one place I
always recall was performing in an outdoor arena
in Israel. We couldn't rehearse on the stage until
the sun had set as our lino floor would otherwise
melt with the heat. On one humid night, with
the stage open to the stars and with the very
dramatic backdrop of the Mediterranean
sea behind us, my pointe shoes started to
disintegrate. I had one pair of pointe shoes
ready for each act but halfway through Act 3,
and facing the 32 fouettés, my shoes literally had
turned to putty and I couldn't change them. This
normally only happens in one's nightmares but
I just managed to complete the fouettés with
tears of pain in my eyes.

Swan Lake

After my first two shows I did have the extraordinarily fortunate experience of being coached by Dame Margot Fonteyn. She was a little bit terrifying because I was expecting her to be smiley and she wasn't. She gave me valuable insights into playing the role. In particular, she explained that you should always be a woman first but with the mannerisms of a swan and also that every single move you make should be part of the narrative. She didn't correct any of my technique but instead spent time exploring Odette's sensitivities and Odile's seductive charm. In both of these photos I am partnered by the wonderful Roberto Bolle. In the middle of Act 3 (opposite) I'm holding this famous balance which creates a lot of excitement as you near the climatic end of the pas de deux. By this time, the black swan Odile makes sure she has complete power over her prince.

Swan Lake

Darcey came into my life in 1988. I think she was 19 at the time and like a beautiful racehorse. We went on to work together for almost 20 years until the day that she retired. At first considered a purely classical dancer, she developed into an artiste of great range.

DONALD MACLEARY (COACH FOR 20 YEARS)

Swan Lake
SEPTEMBER, 1992
ANTHONY CRICKMAY'S STUDIO, LONDON

One of the best dance photographers I ever worked with, I always wanted to impress Anthony Crickmay. He had an innate ability to understand the dancer's body and knowledge of the work that was necessary to try to create any move. I did many fashion shoots with him but the best were always the dance photo shoots. He was able to extract the most flattering shots – his timing of catching a lift or a jump was remarkable and he would nearly always be flat on the floor, lying on his stomach, to take the shot. On this shoot we spent about four hours creating different moves. Photographed with my dashing Hungarian partner Zoltan Solymosi, this is one of the first lifts of the Black Swan *pas de deux*.

Polaroid ® L9V0133

Swan Lake

FEBRUARY, 2000

THE ROYAL BALLET, COVENT GARDEN, LONDON

——

This photo by Mario Testino was taken backstage at the Royal Opera House, with the lighting rigs down. I had been rehearsing all day and Janine Limberg from the Press Department was trying to squeeze in 20 minutes for Mario to photograph me. Normally you'd leave four hours for him. I took 10 minutes to do my own make-up. Mario thought that I hadn't done a bad job at all, given it was stage make-up and I had taken an hour less than a normal make-up artist at one of his shoots. In addition, we had no stylist and the shoot took just 10 minutes. It is probably one of the most popular posters of The Royal Ballet Company – a testimony to Mario's fantastic talent.

The Nutcracker
31 DECEMBER, 1999
THE ROYAL BALLET, COVENT GARDEN, LONDON

In one of the five studios at the Royal Opera House with Roberto Bolle and my friend, mentor and coach Donald MacLeary. Donald coached me in nearly all my roles from the age of 19 up to my retirement. He had exceptional musicality and always said that the most simple and pure lines created the best effect, and he was right. I loved his style and discipline and cannot thank him enough for the hours and hours we spent together. These photos were taken on New Year's Eve 1999. Roberto and I had the first show of the new century the next day and these were also the first shows Roberto and I had ever done together. His English was very limited and my Italian was non-existent, but this didn't bother us as we were able to communicate through the movement and the music.

Words cannot do justice to Darcey's extraordinary talent and beauty. With her perfect classical proportions, warmth of personality and dazzling technique, she excelled in all the great ballerina roles, whether it be classical or modern, dramatic or just pure dance.

SIR PETER WRIGHT (CHOREOGRAPHER/DIRECTOR)

The Nutcracker

DECEMBER, 1999

THE ROYAL BALLET, COVENT GARDEN, LONDON

Getting ready for the Sugar Plum Fairy role was never easy, having to wait all evening just to come on to do the climactic last 15 minutes of the show. Timing was everything. Trying not to get ready too early, warm up too early and get on the stage too early was a challenge. I always had a little of that sick feeling in my stomach before I went on, knowing that by the end of coda I wouldn't be able to feel my legs or feet.

The Nutcracker

DECEMBER, 1999

THE ROYAL BALLET, COVENT GARDEN, LONDON

Sir Peter Wright's beautiful production seems to never age. Set to Tchaikovsky's music, Peter made sure that in Act 3 the Principal couple really were the icing on the cake. To the audience it looks like one of the most simple and stylish roles, but real stamina was required. If the conductor did not play the music too fast I was able to give every step its true value from the port de bras to the tip of my pointe shoe, and this made it really enjoyable. In the *pas de deux* I am partnered by Roberto Bolle.

Manon

JULY, 1998

THE ROYAL BALLET, COVENT GARDEN, LONDON

———

Choreographed by Sir Kenneth MacMillan,
Manon premiered in 1974. I enjoyed *Manon*
every single time I danced it because it is so
dramatically rewarding. *Manon* was not taxing
technically, but what was most important was
having the ability to portray Manon's life from a
young, innocent girl to an experienced lover and
then to a dying woman.

Manon

JULY, 1998

THE ROYAL BALLET, COVENT GARDEN, LONDON

In this rehearsal at the end of Act 1, Manon is seduced by wealth, which she finds totally irresistible. I am rehearsing the subtleties of the role as Manon realises her allure to other men and thereby her ability to get what she wants. The role of the wealthy man, Monsieur G.M., is played here by Christopher Saunders.

Manon

FEBRUARY, 1992

THE ROYAL BALLET, COVENT GARDEN, LONDON

It is very enjoyable playing opposite all the many characters in this ballet. This scene from Act 1 shows Adam Cooper as my brother, Lescaut, who has plays a pivotal role in Manon's life by leading her down the wrong path. Adam was perfectly devious in this role.

Manon

NOVEMBER, 2005

THE ROYAL BALLET, COVENT GARDEN, LONDON

The first main *pas de deux* of the ballet is an extraordinary choreographic work describing the excitement of young love using both technical and fluent movements. Set to the beautiful music of Massenet, Sir Kenneth used pauses within the piece to express the attraction of their first meeting but it did also allow us to catch our breath. I'm pictured here with Roberto Bolle playing Des Grieux.

Manon
NOVEMBER, 2005
THE ROYAL BALLET, COVENT GARDEN, LONDON

In his *pas de deuxs*, Sir Kenneth had the ability to create an intimate conversation. The entwined moves between the dancers speaks to the audience with such clarity that the narrative is easy to understand. Within the bedroom *pas de deux* there are many off-balance promenades and lifts that you have to throw yourself into. This was easy for me to do as Roberto was so assured as a partner.

In the complex trio with Monsieur G.M. and Lescaut, my brother is convincing me not to follow my heart and instead be with the older, richer man.

Manon

I can only imagine this ballet ever being choreographed by the genius Sir Kenneth MacMillan. Each act moulds seamlessly together. With music by Massenet and designs by Nicholas Georgiadis, Sir Kenneth produced a work that I believe will never be bettered. In the final act, Manon and Des Grieux are reunited in the most desperate of circumstances. When I danced this scene, the choreography made me feel their pain and hopelessness. At the end of this ballet there was rarely a dry eye in the house.

The Sleeping Beauty

MARCH, 2003

THE ROYAL BALLET, COVENT GARDEN, LONDON

The Sleeping Beauty is probably The Royal Ballet's signature classic ballet. On the right, I am performing the Act 1 solo and on the left is the awakening scene and shows the joy that the spell has been broken. Strangely, I never really wanted to do *Beauty*, although ironically I ended up performing four different productions over my career. This is Natasha Makarova's production. *Beauty* didn't get any easier, it was always a long and difficult work, but I enjoyed the challenge and learnt to take risks to create excitement. As Princess Aurora I often felt that I did the whole ballet in the first act, as I never seemed to stop dancing. For every show I would have at least four pairs of pointe shoes ready as I didn't know whether a single pair would last an Act. I have memories of once suffering from back spasms during the Rose Adage and also having a cramp in my hamstring. The joy of a long three-act ballet!

The Sleeping Beauty
MARCH, 2003
THE ROYAL BALLET, COVENT GARDEN, LONDON

The celebrated Act 3 *pas de deux*. I'm partnered
by Roberto Bolle.

The Sleeping Beauty

MARCH, 2003

THE ROYAL BALLET, COVENT GARDEN, LONDON

The sense of achievement never waned upon reaching Act 3. It is a beautiful end to a ballet, with its grand style and the feeling that it was very much an 'Imperial' ballet. At over 3 hours long, there would always be something you were not going to be completely happy with, such as a turn or a balance. One of the ways you are rewarded for your efforts was by the choreographic celebration of the marriage in the *pas de deux*, solo and coda. This pose, known as a fish dive, cannot be held for long as you are holding on to your partner with only your right leg. I couldn't help but smile at my Prince even with the pain.

The Sleeping Beauty

APRIL, 1994

THE KENNEDY CENTER, WASHINGTON DC, USA

This was the dress rehearsal for the premiere of Sir Anthony Dowell's new production of *The Sleeping Beauty* in Washington. Apart from the anxiety of not opening at home and knowing that President Clinton was coming to watch the premiere, a lot of things had been going wrong in rehearsals. The lino was slippery, the costumes were more elaborate than we were used to, and we hadn't been able to rehearse with the set until three days before we left for Washington.

The picture on the right shows my sense of relief at having got through it all. Well, either relief or pain. I vividly remember the first night. Due to the fact we had the Clintons watching there was a lot of security in the theatre. I forgot my security pass when coming onto the stage before the first act and as I went through the metal detector the security guard told me that I had to have my pass. Having no time to go back to my dressing room, I had to convince him that I really was Aurora and was needed on stage.

The Sleeping Beauty

APRIL, 1994

THE KENNEDY CENTER, WASHINGTON DC, USA

Pictured In the wings with a nervous smile on my face before my Act 1 entrance of the stage rehearsal.

Romeo and Juliet

OCTOBER, 1993

THE ROYAL BALLET, COVENT GARDEN, LONDON

Juliet was one of my favourite roles, as you are an actress first and then a dancer. When Sir Kenneth MacMillan first gave me the opportunity to play Juliet in his ballet, I did know that my Director, Sir Anthony Dowell, was not that confident in me playing this role because of my height. He did compliment me afterwards by saying that I made the role my own. I'm pictured here with Jonathan Cope, in the Ballroom *pas de deux*. This is the magical first meeting of Romeo and Juliet. Sir Kenneth's choreography ensured a great feeling of electricity between us. In the solo, pictured on the right, I get to show Juliet's naivety, and as there is really only one technically difficult step I had the opportunity to get carried away by Prokofiev's music. My very first role in *Romeo and Juliet* was alongside Nureyev as one of the three main Harlots. He had come to perform in a gala performance in honour of Dame Margot Fonteyn. Even that evening he kept the curtain waiting as he went through his steps on the stage in his famous gold clogs.

Romeo and Juliet

Dancers of Bussell's ability emerge only once in a decade. She will be an international star. She can do anything you throw at her, upside down and back to front.

SIR KENNETH MACMILLAN (CHOREOGRAPHER)

Romeo and Juliet
OCTOBER, 1993
THE ROYAL BALLET, COVENT GARDEN, LONDON

As a student I remember always running to the wings to get a spot to watch the Principals dance the Balcony *pas de deux*. One of the most brilliantly moulded *pas de deux*, it grows and builds as Romeo and Juliet discover the extent of their love for each other. This photo is of the solo within the *pas de deux*. Juliet was a role where I was able to forget about my technique and just let the music lead me. Prokofiev's score is so powerful. Over the years, when I was on my own on stage at the beginning of Act 3, I would lose myself in the story and well up with tears. Sometimes I forgot that there was even an audience watching.

3

Selected Repertoire

Requiem

OCTOBER, 2004

THE ROYAL BALLET, COVENT GARDEN, LONDON

First premiered in 1976 and dedicated to the
memory of his mentor John Cranko, this Sir
Kenneth MacMillan piece is like no other. Every
step is so distinctive to *Requiem*. The shapes
you create either with the arms behind you or
the hand against the face have such meaning
within this modern ballet. The extraordinary
atmosphere of the work was felt not only by
the entire audience but also by the dancers.
I danced the solo role, Agnus Dei.

Requiem

OCTOBER, 2004

THE ROYAL BALLET, COVENT GARDEN, LONDON

Inspired by the paintings of William Blake and
set to Faure's ethereal *Requiem*, the masterly
choreography ensures that every dancer
internalises Kenneth's sorrow. I felt this sorrow
every single time I performed it. Carlos Acosta is
dancing the role of the Offertoire boy.

Raymonda
NOVEMBER, 1998
THE ROYAL BALLET, COVENT GARDEN, LONDON

Regarded as Petipa's last true masterpiece,
I always felt I was dancing in the Mariinsky
Theatre itself when I performed this ballet. It
is very appropriate that I am dancing here with
my partner, the Kirov star Igor Zelensky. There
is such a sense of pride within *Raymonda's*
distinctive style. This act features the celebration
of a wedding and much of the dancing is of
Hungarian character. At the end of the piece
there are at least 20 retirés that start off slow and
get faster and faster. It was so satisfying when
everything went right and you were in sync with
the conductor... it built such excitement.

Giselle

MAY, 1995

THE ROYAL BALLET, COVENT GARDEN, LONDON

One of the most famous romantic ballets, I am
dancing Sir Peter Wright's production. In the first
Act of this two-act ballet, Giselle's love of dance
and her fragility are dramatically contrasted.
She is deceived by her love, the Count Albrecht
(danced by Jonathan Cope) and this leads to her
madness and tragic death of a broken heart. It is
a rare occurrence within the classics to express
so freely and I did always enjoy finding the
realism within the mad scene (opposite). When
my daughter Phoebe first saw this scene where I
die at the end, she turned to the people next to
her and reassured them that I was alright, and
that I was just resting before the next act.

Giselle

MAY, 1995

THE ROYAL BALLET, COVENT GARDEN, LONDON

As far as I was concerned *Giselle* was always
about Act 2. The choreography was a joy
to perform. The light jumps and the unique
partnering illustrated beautifully that Giselle was
now a spirit. I couldn't help but want to perfect
this illusion, and however tiring Act 2 was, I
never wanted it to end.

La Bayadère

MARCH, 1997

THE ROYAL BALLET, COVENT GARDEN, LONDON

Dancing Nikiya in Makarova's production of *La Bayadère* is a beautiful role as it is authentically feminine. Nikiya is a temple girl and in the Act 1 snake solo (pictured), she tries to win back her love, the Prince. The sustained balance in this arabesque is repeated three times. The conductor knows exactly what you are trying to achieve and will help you by stretching out the music to sustain each balance. In the original *La Bayadère*, Minkus' music and Petipa's choreography were created together, so they are truly entwined. To get the best from the choreography you must have an excellent relationship with your conductor. The first and third Acts have wonderful costumes with bare midrifts. I would sometimes stick a jewel in my belly button using wig glue, but it would nearly always fly out in a turn or as I was being partnered.

Cinderella

JANUARY, 1993

THE ROYAL BALLET, COVENT GARDEN, LONDON

Cinderella was the first three-act British ballet
(premiered in 1948) and is one of my favourite
ballets by Sir Frederick Ashton. This lyrical classic
has musicality, excellent timing of the comedy
and pure, clean choreography which makes
it as enjoyable for the dancers as it is for the
audience. I always had a lot of fun as Cinderella
in rags, but it was the second act solo which
I enjoyed the most. This solo finishes with a
double ménage, where you go around the stage
twice whilst turning. As the music picks up
pace, the faster and more impressive the turns
become, so I always ended up with a dizzy blur
of lights in front of my eyes. To be still at the end
of the solo was really challenging.

Checkmate

JUNE, 1993

THE ROYAL BALLET, COVENT GARDEN, LONDON

This is one of Dame Ninette De Valois' most significant works, which premiered in 1937. It is a timeless piece and features the famous Black Queen solo. This powerful and seductive role creates an extraordinary fear on stage. The Queen turns her daggers threatening to kill the red King whilst never actually touching him. I was fortunate enough to be coached by the wonderful Dame Beryl Grey, who had joined the Company just four years later in 1941. The Black Queen was considered one of Beryl's iconic roles and she remembers every detail and feeling that De Valois wanted from her ballet. I loved having a role that was so evil and whilst I usually disliked props, the curling motion that the Black Queen makes with the daggers really enhances the drama. The chess board floor accentuates the distance the Queen had to travel across the stage, which made it quite exhausting.

Have you seen Darcey dance? She is beautiful in every conceivable way. Physically beautiful, but also genuinely, spiritually beautiful. And she's a phenomenal dancer.

TWYLA THARP (CHOREOGRAPHER)

Push Comes to Shove
FEBRUARY, 1997

THE ROYAL BALLET, COVENT GARDEN, LONDON

Like so much of Twyla Tharp's famous repertoire, *Push Comes to Shove* (which first premiered in 1976) contains a loose-limbed jazz influence style. This gives classically trained dancers a different performing attitude and I really enjoyed dancing this cool, distinctive work. I was also very fortunate to have spent three months in 1995 with Twyla creating the three-act ballet *Mr Worldy Wise*, with Irek Mukhamedov. Based loosely on the life of Rossini, it didn't just have the art of ballet but also the influence of Broadway entertainment.

Awakening pas de deux

NOVEMBER, 2004

THE ROYAL BALLET, COVENT GARDEN, LONDON

A lyrical and romantic work choreographed by
Sir Frederick Ashton. It captures the romance
of the Prince and Aurora meeting for the first
time. You can tell that Jonathan Cope and myself
are from the same training as we are hitting
the identical pose. In this picture below, we are
exiting the stage directly towards a bright light
while we sustained a series of balances together.
The problem was looking into the blinding
spotlight which made us think we might hit the
wings on the way out.

Awakening pas de deux

NOVEMBER, 2004

A Month in the Country

JUNE, 2005

THE ROYAL BALLET, COVENT GARDEN, LONDON

Essentially a ballet within a play, I had always wanted to dance this role. Based on Ivan Turgenev's play, it is a moving portrait of an older woman, Natalya Petrovna, hopelessly attracted to a younger man. You simply cannot fault this work by Sir Frederick Ashton. Created on Sir Anthony Dowell and Lynn Seymour, Sir Fred certainly used her exceptional dramatic abilities. In the solo on the left, he wanted as much movement from the upper body as possible, to such an extent that it was very easy to lose your balance.

A Month in the Country

JUNE, 2005

THE ROYAL BALLET, COVENT GARDEN, LONDON

I danced this role later in my career and I felt it was perfect timing for me. My partner, Rupert Pennefather was almost 15 years my junior. The ballet has such an incredibly sad ending. Set in an era with rigid rules of social behavior, Natalya and the young tutor come to realise their personal tragedy of not being able to be with one another.

Sylvia

NOVEMBER, 2004

THE ROYAL BALLET, COVENT GARDEN, LONDON

I shared my dressing room with fellow Principal and good friend Miyako Yoshida, and the messy side is hers! Having my hair done by the wonderful Melanie for the three-act ballet *Sylvia* took just over half an hour. After doing my make-up, which also took half an hour, I would go to the studio to warm up for 45 minutes and work in my pointe shoes that I had prepared the day before. I would then get into my costume and make sure I was on stage at least 15 minutes before the curtain went up. I always had to get a feel of the stage and the lighting, and go through my entrances and exits and any step I wanted to practice.

Sylvia

NOVEMBER, 2004

THE ROYAL BALLET, COVENT GARDEN, LONDON

In 2004, The Royal Ballet brought back *Sylvia* after an absence of almost 40 years. Choreographed by Sir Frederick Ashton, this ballet premiered in 1952 and was created on Dame Margot Fonteyn and Michael Soames. It took many months of collaboration to recreate this three-act ballet. Much of the notation was missing and there was only some old archive film footage of Margot Fonteyn and Nadia Nerina dancing Sylvia. This was a very difficult rehearsal process as we had to breathe life back into this work, but fortunately it was a great success.

Sylvia

Based on a Roman myth, Sylvia is a demi-god and a nymph of Diana's. It is an exhausting first act with many athletic jumps, which is unusual for Ashton's choreography. This is the first encounter between Sylvia and the shepherd Aminta, who is a mortal. Sylvia falls in love with Aminta even though she is not permitted to do so by Diana.

Sylvia

NOVEMBER, 2004

THE ROYAL BALLET, COVENT GARDEN, LONDON

Photographs taken from the wings during Act 1.

Darcey's beauty was evident both as a dancer and as a person. Since the first time we danced together, she gave me the strength to face the Opera House stage and to deal with the pressure and emotions.

ROBERTO BOLLE (PRINCIPAL DANCER)

Sylvia

NOVEMBER, 2004

THE ROYAL BALLET, COVENT GARDEN, LONDON

It was always a rush to get ready between Acts so that you could have a little time on the stage before the curtain went up. Between Acts we often changed hair, pointe shoes and costume. I am getting ready outside my dressing room for the Act 3 celebrations of *Sylvia*. I am wearing an extraordinary tutu with elaborate gold braid that weighed it down, which did not help with the amount of jumps and lifts we had to do.

Sylvia

NOVEMBER, 2004

THE ROYAL BALLET, COVENT GARDEN, LONDON

Pictured with Jonathan Cope in the impressive entrance of the *pas de deux* in Act 3, which celebrates the marriage of Sylvia and Aminta. To prepare for this lift I would climb up a ladder in the wings. It is an unnerving lift, with most of the weight taken by my knee on his shoulder and his right hand in the centre of my back. The hardest technical aspect is coming down from it smoothly on stage.

Sylvia

NOVEMBER, 2004

THE ROYAL BALLET, COVENT GARDEN, LONDON

———

I had two wonderful partners in the years that
I did this role. I first premiered it with Jonathan
Cope, but later I was partnered by Roberto Bolle.
Roberto, a Guest Principal from La Scala in Milan,
was my main partner for the last seven years of
my career. Sir Frederick Ashton's choreography
and musicality created some exceptional and
technical steps in Act 3 and it is accompanied
by the most memorable part of Léo Delibes'
exquisite score. I found I had to be incredibly
focused to achieve the best from this technically
challenging *pas de deux*.

Sylvia

NOVEMBER, 2004

THE ROYAL BALLET, COVENT GARDEN, LONDON

The relief of making your last entrance for
a well-received ballet was almost palpable.
Suddenly my body didn't feel as bad as it did
midway through the performance! If I was happy
that everything went well and that the audience
really enjoyed it, I would smile even more.

Balanchine

SYMPHONY IN C
BALLET IMPERIAL
THE FOUR TEMPERAMENTS
APOLLO
STRAVINSKY VIOLIN CONCERTO

Symphony in C

APRIL, 1997

THE ROYAL BALLET, COVENT GARDEN, LONDON

Created by George Balanchine as a showcase for the talent of his whole Company, this one-act ballet is set around the four Principal couples. My role was the Adagio, which was one of the most controlled adagios I think I ever performed. I remember a funny incident involving our Director, Sir Anthony Dowell. He had commissioned new costumes and five minutes before the curtain went up he was checking his dancers. He grabbed my headdress with one hand and yanked it further forward. I had to run into the wings and re-pin the whole thing with a minute to go... our Director always wanted us to look our best!

Symphony in C

APRIL, 1997

THE ROYAL BALLET, COVENT GARDEN, LONDON

I would almost shake trying to sustain the duration of the arabesque when holding Jonathan's one hand. Of course our aim was to make it look as though it was the easiest move. If the conductor was enjoying the adagio it could become agonisingly slow and this photo reminds me of the pain that I was hiding.

Symphony in C

APRIL, 1997

THE ROYAL BALLET, COVENT GARDEN, LONDON

The last sustained pose at the end of the Second
Movement of *Symphony in C*. it was always an
art for Jonathan to get me out of this position
gracefully for our bow.

Symphony in C

Ballet Imperial

FEBRUARY, 2006

THE ROYAL BALLET, COVENT GARDEN, LONDON

Set to Tchaikovsky's Piano Concerto No. 2, this one-act piece is Balanchine's tribute to the classical style of his roots at the Mariinsky Theatre. It is one of Balanchine's works that requires a huge amount of stamina and by the end you just can't feel your legs. I am partnered here by Rupert Pennefather. This would have been a much more enjoyable role if I hadn't had to wear this brand-new gold lamé tutu! The Soloist role, which I have also danced, has a beautiful black velvet tutu.

The Four Temperaments

NOVEMBER, 2006

THE ROYAL BALLET, COVENT GARDEN, LONDON

I was very fortunate to have danced many
of Balanchine's works and I believe *The Four
Temperaments* is the most true to his imagery.
From your very first step you create the style
that can only be Balanchine's choreography.
His works that feature the minimalist leotards
and tights really showcase the extraordinary
foresight and excitement that he bought to
modern ballet. I'm pictured with Carlos Acosta.

Apollo

APRIL, 2003

THE ROYAL BALLET, COVENT GARDEN, LONDON

Looking out at the auditorium before the arrival of the audience for a performance of Apollo. These photos were taken by Bryan Adams, and on the left you can see my very dear friend Janine Limberg, who worked for The Royal Ballet, assisting Bryan. There was always a buzz of anticipation before any show, but I never felt real pressure before I performed *Apollo* as I always enjoyed it and felt natural. This was true for most of George Balanchine's work.

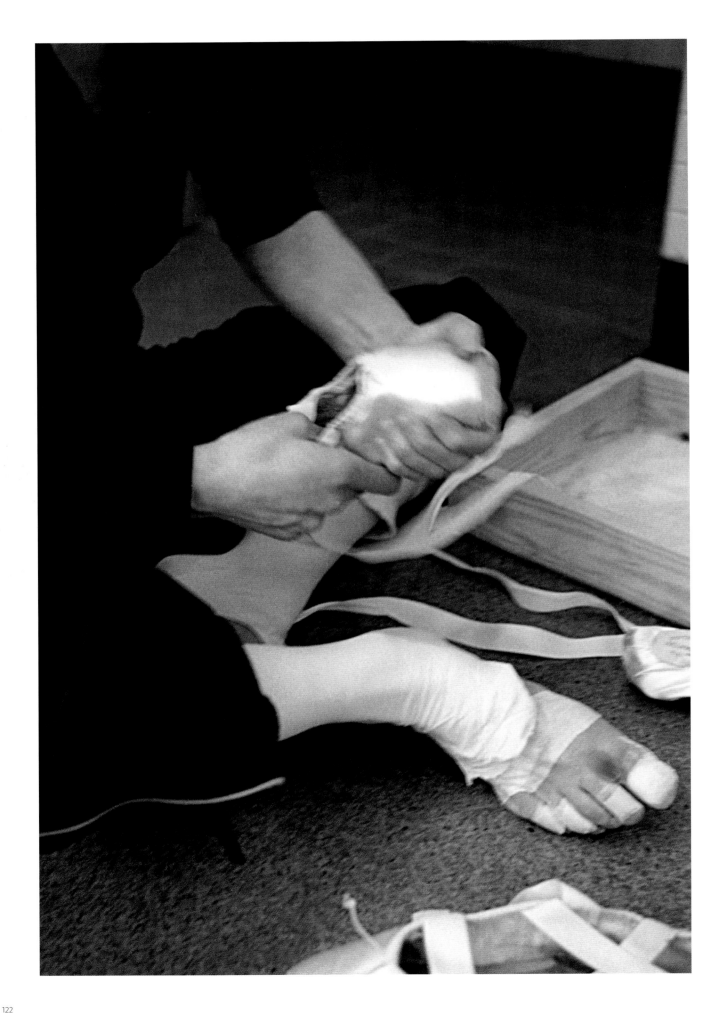

Apollo

APRIL, 2003

THE ROYAL BALLET, COVENT GARDEN, LONDON

Protecting my feet for the performance ahead.
I individually bandaged each toe so that I didn't
get too many blisters. I have always felt this must
be similar to strapping a boxer's hands.

After about 10 years I was able to apply my
stage make-up in 30 minutes. It was all about
accentuating the eyes and the lips for the
audience to see our expressions more clearly.
False eyelashes were a must.

Apollo

APRIL, 2003
THE ROYAL BALLET, COVENT GARDEN, LONDON

Arguably George Balanchine's signature work, *Apollo* premiered in 1928. A one-act ballet set to the score by Stravinsky, it is the first example of his neoclassical ballet, with the dance, costumes and set all in minimalist form. Terpsichore, the chosen muse of Apollo, was the most beautifully rewarding role to dance because it has such clarity and I never tired of trying to perfect the seamless lines. Bryan Adams put himself in the front wing of the stage and he captured the essence of the ballet perfectly. I am pictured here with Carlos Acosta.

Apollo

APRIL, 2003

THE ROYAL BALLET, COVENT GARDEN, LONDON

The shapes that are created within this ballet are
so distinctive, they are completely true to both
Apollo's learning and the strong control he has
over his three muses. Carlos Acosta played
this brilliantly.

Stravinsky Violin Concerto

OCTOBER, 2006

THE ROYAL BALLET, COVENT GARDEN, LONDON

One of George Balanchine's later works, *Violin Concerto* premiered in 1972. It features two strongly contrasting Principal *pas de deuxs*. The *pas de deux* I'm rehearsing here with Edward Watson was the more gymnastic of the two and featured a series of walkovers. You had to make sure you were very flexible before you started any rehearsal.

Stravinsky Violin Concerto

OCTOBER, 2006

THE ROYAL BALLET, COVENT GARDEN, LONDON

In performance with Edward Watson, walking through the air. I think Ed and I would have been compatible for many more Balanchine works because we were both flexible and strong, which suits this style of choreography, but unfortunately I retired soon afterwards.

Stravinsky Violin Concerto

5

Created Works

Darcey was this incredibly gifted ballerina and a true star in every sense of the word – at no time did she ever play the diva. Her creative work was intensely inspiring due to her possessing the most physically capable body of any dancer of her generation.

JONATHAN COPE (PRINCIPAL DANCER AND COACH, THE ROYAL BALLET COMPANY)

Spirit of Fugue
NOVEMBER, 1988
THE ROYAL BALLET, COVENT GARDEN, LONDON
——

My first created work was with David Bintley, who is Director of the Birmingham Royal Ballet. Aged 19 at the time, I had only been at The Royal Ballet Company for two months. It was extraordinary to be working with another top choreographer in these early days. Sir Kenneth MacMillan was quite cross, as I was moved by him into the Company to create *The Prince of* *the Pagodas*, and he felt that this took time away from his rehearsals. I also knew how fortunate I was to be working for the first time with *the* Jonathan Cope. He was a leading Principal and I was a new soloist, after only having the one year in the *corps de ballet*. A very cool and abstract piece, I enjoyed being the mysterious new dancer in the Company.

The Prince of the Pagodas

DECEMBER, 1989

THE ROYAL BALLET, COVENT GARDEN, LONDON

The premiere of *The Prince of the Pagodas* was delayed because of Sir Kenneth's illness, so we rehearsed for nearly a year. I had no idea how extraordinary it was to be intimately working with such a renowned choreographer for this amount of time. Jonny and I were working on three *pas de deuxs* that Sir Kenneth kept changing and changing. I would often look at Jonny and wonder which version we were going to do that day. Quite often we mistakenly mixed them up. Everything was so new to me, besides *Pagodas* I was also learning a whole new repertoire after moving from Sadler's Wells Royal Ballet. We are photographed in the old rehearsal studios at Baron's Court. The picture on the right shows Jonny pushing me through the air in a very high *fouetté en l'air*.

The Prince of the Pagodas

DECEMBER, 1989

THE ROYAL BALLET, COVENT GARDEN, LONDON

Princess Rose was meant to be a young girl who was inexperienced in life, which is one of the reasons Sir Kenneth picked me from the *corps de ballet* as a new young talent. This meant I could be myself. Set to the music of Benjamin Britten, *The Prince of the Pagodas* was an extraordinary work as it was essentially three classical ballets in one. It was a marathon of a ballet and I had four challenging solos. Not only this, but my Director played the role of my father, the King. It was daunting to know that Sir Anthony Dowell was going be on the throne and scrutinise my technique every night.

The first time I worked with Darcey was when Kenneth MacMillan created the very challenging role of Princess Rose for her in The Prince of the Pagodas. She had just joined The Royal Ballet and her unique physical qualities were already remarkable.

DAME MONICA MASON (DIRECTOR, THE ROYAL BALLET COMPANY)

The Prince of the Pagodas

DECEMBER, 1989

THE ROYAL BALLET, COVENT GARDEN, LONDON

The Second Act tells the story of Princess Rose's dream. In addition to the second main *pas de deux* with Jonathan, I had four extra-short *pas de deuxs* with my four Suitors. I don't remember coming off stage at all for the whole of this Act. As we had a lot of time to rehearse this work, Sir Kenneth MacMillan was able to create moves that hadn't been done before. He did not want these four *pas de deuxs* to look easy, as the Suitors are quite rough and crude, so it was physically exhausting for me. In this photo I am with one of the Princes, Bruce Sansom.

The Prince of the Pagodas

DECEMBER, 1989
THE ROYAL BALLET, COVENT GARDEN, LONDON

The marriage celebration in Act 3 was a return to the beautiful curves and lines of a true classical ballet. Sir Kenneth had chosen a strong cast which included five Principal men and Principal Fiona Chadwick, who played my Step-Sister. I would not have managed without their experience and support. On the first night of this production, I danced my first three-act ballet, which had also been created on me. At the end of the show, and whilst the Company was still on stage, our Director Sir Anthony Dowell promoted me to Principal. I recall that all I managed to say was 'are you sure?'.

Winter Dreams

FEBRUARY, 1991

THE ROYAL BALLET, COVENT GARDEN, LONDON

Sir Kenneth MacMillan was instrumental in my career. He believed in me as a dancer and gave me confidence at a young age. I would never have had the career that I had, if not for Sir Kenneth's vision. It was his doing to move me from Sadler's Wells Royal Ballet to the resident Company, The Royal Ballet, in order to create *The Prince of the Pagodas* and then *Winter Dreams*. It was an extraordinary time in my life and I will never forget him. *Winter Dreams* was based on Chekov's *Three Sisters*, and when creating the role of Masha, Sir Kenneth always wanted to see how I would interpret the character. He was often very quiet and would only correct me if he thought I was going down the wrong path.

Winter Dreams

FEBRUARY, 1991

THE ROYAL BALLET, COVENT GARDEN, LONDON

Winter Dreams was first performed as a 10-minute *pas de deux*, created for myself and the great Bolshoi star, Irek Mukhamedov, when he first joined the Company. It premiered at the Palladium in July 1990 for Her Majesty Queen Elizabeth The Queen Mother's 90th birthday and it was called the *Farewell pas de deux*. Kenneth insisted on extracting real emotions and tried to instill in me a life's worth of experience when I was only 21. He did take me aside after a rehearsal and said that Irek was giving 100 per cent passion as Vershinin, my lover, and I was only giving 50 per cent as Masha... I was shocked but I understood him perfectly.

Winter Dreams

MAY, 2007

FAREWELL PERFORMANCES,
SADLER'S WELLS THEATRE, LONDON

Whilst this was made on myself and the Russian Principal Irek Mukhamedov, I consider myself fortunate to have performed this exquisite *pas de deux* with handsome partners of many different nationalities. My last performances were with the Italian, Roberto Bolle. Roberto's strength and fluidity bought yet another style to Kenneth's great choreography. This was one of the ballets made on me that really felt part of me, and I always enjoyed performing it.

Winter Dreams

MAY, 2007

FAREWELL PERFORMANCES,
SADLER'S WELLS THEATRE, LONDON

The *pas de deux* became a one-act ballet which was first performed on 7th February, 1991. The role of my husband was originally played by the Director of The Royal Ballet, Sir Anthony Dowell. It was extraordinary to not only dance with my Director in my early years but to gain so much throughout my career from his unique eye and knowledge. I had a tremendous respect for Anthony as both a dancer and Director. Pictured here in 2007 during a stage rehearsal, Anthony is instructing Jonathan Cope on the role he created in 1991.

Winter Dreams

MAY, 2007

FAREWELL PERFORMANCES,
SADLER'S WELLS THEATRE, LONDON

My last performances at Sadler's Wells Theatre were extremely special as I started my career in this theatre. Many members of the cast were old friends who had been with me throughout my career. Both Jonathan Cope and Nicola Tranah came out of retirement for these shows, and the wonderful Philip Gammon was the pianist again. I'm pictured backstage with Sir Kenneth's wife, Lady Deborah MacMillan, who was always a great support to me.

What makes a ballerina like Darcey? A ballerina has a fragrance that lingers after they have left the stage, leaving an indelible impression on your consciousness. I think I created a short ballet that captured part of Darcey's true essence as a ballerina.

CHRISTOPHER WHEELDON (CHOREOGRAPHER)

Pavane pour une infante dèfunte
OCTOBER, 1996
THE ROYAL BALLET, COVENT GARDEN, LONDON

It was exciting to create this work because I first knew Christopher Wheeldon from The Royal Ballet school when he was eleven and I was thirteen. This was his first commission for The Royal Ballet Company. Not just a *pas de deux* but a full Gala work, it featured a beautifully designed giant lily that hung from the lighting rig above centre stage.

Pavane pour une infante dèfunte

OCTOBER, 1996

THE ROYAL BALLET, COVENT GARDEN, LONDON

Chris wanted me to portray the image of Grace Kelly. The ballet started with me in a long dress, which Jonny had to unravel. I did feel like we were on a movie set. I could imagine Jonny as my Cary Grant. Set to the stunning music by Ravel, the work was difficult in that you had to be incredibly smooth all the way through. The adagio featured a lot of one-handed promenades where the hand was either holding my neck or my shoulder, when it is usually on the waist. I admired the fact that Chris used our skills to the full and I am thrilled that *Pavane* became such a signature piece, which we performed nearly everywhere.

Tryst

MAY, 2002

THE ROYAL BALLET, COVENT GARDEN, LONDON

Tryst was the third work that Christopher Wheeldon created on Jonathan Cope and myself. Rehearsals were nearly always two hours in length and were intensely focused as we were creating a new piece. At this point in our careers, and knowing Chris so well, we were able to contribute to the creative process without any inhibitions. This made the rehearsals incredibly enjoyable as the three of us knew we wanted to create moves that we had never done before. Sometimes I do think that Chris would have preferred us to have been a little less vocal and left the choreographing to him! I remember how particularly physically strong Jonathan was within this piece.

Tryst

MAY, 2002

THE ROYAL BALLET, COVENT GARDEN, LONDON

Set to music by James MacMillan, this was a successful contemporary work, with a high degree of difficulty to execute. This suited Jonny and I as we wanted to be challenged and push ourselves in performances. We embraced the moves that were off-balance and risky, and the stage lighting added to the complexity as it really contrasted with the studio.

Tanglewood
NOVEMBER, 2005
THE ROYAL BALLET, COVENT GARDEN, LONDON

Alastair Marriott and I were in the same year at school, so there were no barriers when it came to creating something new and different. It is intense when there are six men and yourself, as opposed to a *pas de deux* where there are just the two of you. With the responsibility shared across six men, there were some incidents in rehearsal when a mistake was made and it was apparently nobody's fault! Alastair finished this piece before the rest of the one-act ballet, which gave us invaluable time for the men to iron out any rough movements. The performances were smooth and I can't remember one thing going wrong, which was a joy.

DGV

NOVEMBER, 2006

THE ROYAL BALLET, COVENT GARDEN, LONDON

—

When creating his ballets, Christopher Wheeldon has an innate knack of drawing out your strengths. He created the one-act abstract ballet *DGV* using nearly the full Company and he included four Principal couples. Set to the powerful music of James MacMillan, *DGV* culminated in a sequence of synchronised moves. In one rehearsal on stage, Chris totally lost his cool with the four couples as we simply weren't together. As we were all Principals, everyone had strong opinions as to who was in the right! Our *pas de deux* was slow and physical and Gary Avis had to bring me on and off stage in a *Giselle* lift. This is something we had to rehearse over and over again so I didn't shake during the smooth elevation and descent. Gary was amazing, I was so surprised that he never complained.

Guesting

Darcey appeared as a guest during three seasons of New York City Ballet, the first during the historic Balanchine Celebration in 1993 – dancing the Agon Pas de Deux. Our audience was thrilled to see her, and all of her performances were beautiful and memorable...

PETER MARTINS (DIRECTOR, NEW YORK CITY BALLET)

Agon

JUNE, 1993

NEW YORK CITY BALLET, THE METROPOLITAN OPERA, NEW YORK

My first experience of guesting was with the New York City Ballet. It is never easy going into a company totally unknown, as you have to immediately prove yourself, but this was not the case with the NYCB. I actually felt like an American dancer, as my physique suited the Balanchine choreography. I loved the energy and the attack of that style of dancing, especially in Agon where the girl was just as powerful as the man, played here by the exceptional Jock Soto. Agon requires both strength and flexibility, as you have to really control the unwinding of the complex positions of the *pas de deux*.

Swan Lake

JUNE, 1994

NEW YORK CITY BALLET, THE METROPOLITAN OPERA, NEW YORK

A one-act *Swan Lake*, not featuring the black swan Odile. This was a unique production and nothing like I had experienced before. True to Balanchine's style, he had reduced the story down to a concentrated and pure form. The Tchaikovsky score felt like it was on fast-forward, and I danced it slower than they would have liked. My established partner, the wonderful Igor Zelensky, was resident at NYCB at the time. It was very apparent that you had to be a fast learner at NYCB. You'd be given one day to learn the piece and perform it the following day. I wasn't allowed my hours and hours of rehearsals here.

Tchaikovsky Pas de Deux

NOVEMBER,1991

PARIS OPERA BALLET, PARIS

This was the first time I performed at the Paris Opera Ballet, where I experienced their large raked stage at the Palais Garnier. Representing The Royal Ballet, it was also the first time that I had danced this exhilarating yet exhausting Gala piece. George Balanchine's choreography had some of the fastest footwork I had experienced and being on the raked stage meant we needed to adjust our balance and lift our eye level for turns so that we didn't fall into the orchestra pit. I danced with the Hungarian star Zoltan Solymosi and despite our nerves, it was a very exciting performance. We were well received by the French audience.

La Bayadère

FEBRUARY,1998

KIROV BALLET, MARIINSKY THEATRE,
ST PETERSBURG

It was a real honour to perform Nikiya with the Kirov Ballet at the world-famous Mariinsky Theatre. It was one of the most atmospheric places I have ever performed. The history is ingrained within the stage itself and I couldn't stop thinking about all the beautiful dancers who had performed there in the past. The opportunity came about because at the time I was dancing with their famous Principal dancer Igor Zelensky. To this day the Kirov is a 200-strong Company that does not need guest artists so it is an extremely rare occurrence for a British dancer to get to dance with the Company. I will never forget the slightly incredulous faces of the Russian dancers who thought I was stealing their shows, and also the famous old wooden raked stage that ensured the rapid disintegration of my pointe shoes.

La Bayadère

FEBRUARY, 1998

AUSTRALIAN BALLET COMPANY, SYDNEY

Fate had it that I travelled directly from the
Mariinsky Theatre in St Petersburg to the
Australian Ballet Company in Melbourne to
perform a different production of *La Bayadère,*
that of Natasha Makarova. I must admit that the
switch from -30°C to plus 30°C did take a day
or so to get used to! The Company was young
and spirited and their lack of complacency was
so refreshing to be part of. I danced with the
talented young Principal Damien Welch and
whilst he had not performed *La Bayadère*
before, you would have never have known it.

Lento

DECEMBER, 1999

HAMBURG BALLET, GERMANY

I joined Hamburg Ballet's long-standing Director John Neumeier and one of its outstanding contemporary dancers, Otto Bubenicek, to create the *pas de deux Lento*. John was in the middle of creating a full three-act ballet and it was extraordinary that he was able to produce *Lento* at the same time. A difficult piece, the pace of the choreography matched the escalating music of Dmitri Shostakovich and it was hard to sustain the constant energy required for this emotive and modern work. Created in just over a week, it was commissioned for The Royal Ballet's 'A Celebration of International Choreography'. I had such a thrilling time watching his very talented Company in their rehearsals. They were a smaller group and they had a natural style and energy that was inspiring.

Le Corsaire

DECEMBER, 2002

THE ROYAL BALLET, COVENT GARDEN, LONDON

Originally choreographed by Mazilier for the Paris Opera in 1856, I performed this truly exciting gala piece all around the world, from Dallas to Tokyo. I remember two performances in particular. One was when I performed in front of the Chinese Premier in Beijing. As he was being filmed watching our performance, there was a light directly on him and so there was no way of missing him in the audience. Afterwards, in perfect English, he did say that he enjoyed it very much. I also remember dancing *Corsaire* with Carlos Acosta at the 75th Anniversary Gala of The Royal Ballet at the Opera House. When performed to its potential, the tension created between the pure classical princess role and the raw athleticism of your partner 'the slave' will often have the audience out of their seats. I think we got close.

Le Corsaire

DECEMBER, 2002

THE ROYAL BALLET, COVENT GARDEN, LONDON

In the middle, somewhat elevated

MARCH, 2002

THE ROYAL BALLET, COVENT GARDEN, LONDON

In the middle was one of my most favourite contemporary pieces to dance. It has an immediate and almost shocking impact from the opening scene. The strength of William Forsythe's choreographic style and the energy of the music by Thom Wilems ensures that it is almost impossible for the audience to take their eyes off it. What Billy wants from his choreography is for the dancer to push out of the realms of their classical form and he certainly achieves this. With the flawless Roberto Bolle as my partner, I was very happy to perform *In the middle* anywhere, not just at the Royal Opera House. I have fond memories of dancing it in many lovely small theatres around Italy on a tour called 'Bolle and friends'.

Sylvia

NOVEMBER, 2005

BUCKINGHAM PALACE, LONDON

On stage in the Ballroom at Buckingham Palace.
HRH Prince of Wales had very kindly allowed this
Gala Performance to be held there in support
of The Royal Ballet School. Fortunately for me,
Jonathan Cope came out of retirement so that
we could do this one-off performance together.
We were quite nervous despite dancing a piece
we knew so well – maybe it was the location.

Le Jeune Homme et la Mort

MARCH, 2006

LA SCALA, MILAN

In rehearsal with Roberto Bolle and the incomparable choreographer Roland Petit. I was invited to perform with La Scala and it was amazing to get to work with Roland himself. He originally choreographed this piece in 1946. Also renowned for his work in Hollywood films, this sexy 80 year old has been a dancer and choreographer for 60 years and he has lost none of his zest. One of the hardest things for me to learn was how to light up a cigarette on stage and smoke and dance at the same time.

Le Jeune Homme et la Mort
MARCH, 2006
LA SCALA, MILAN

This dark, theatrically dramatic one-act ballet has the woman representing death and the man as a tortured artist. Death seduces him into taking his own life. It is an extraordinary role for the man, exhibiting his madness with every athletic move he makes. Roberto Bolle, like all the male dancers who play this role, was mentally and physically exhausted by the end. For my part, I have never played a role of such relentless evil.

Le Jeune Homme et la Mort

MARCH, 2006

LA SCALA, MILAN

The costumes by Cocteau and sets by Georges Wakhévitch add to its dramatic intensity. When first reviewed in the 1940s it was seen as shockingly erotic and it has retained that element. There is no doubt that this work has stood the test of time. Set in the artist's attic studio, I always felt we were part of a film set.

Le Jeune Homme et la Mort

Le Jeune Homme et la Mort

MARCH, 2006

LA SCALA, MILAN

The last scene is set on the rooftops of Paris, and here I am taking instruction after a stage call from the choreographer Roland Petit. The choreographic detail of this piece is very important as it ensures that the subject matter in no way becomes clichéd. I was so fortunate to receive his insight and after performing *Le Jeune* with Roberto in Milan, I went on to perform it with Igor Zelensky at Sadler's Wells Theatre in London. I also filmed it in Japan with the Japanese star Tetsuya Kumakawa.

Charity performance

1998

THE HAYMARKET THEATRE, LONDON

Dawn French approached me to do this piece
and I had no hesitation at all in saying yes as
we had worked together before on *French and
Saunders*. It was easy to choreograph together
as Dawn has a good knowledge of dance and I
actually followed many of her instructions. Dawn
had my costume copied but went to town on
the ballerina's make-up. With Dawn playing my
mirror image you can imagine the most difficult
technique was keeping a straight face. We first
performed this in the Haymarket Theatre for a
charity gala. It went on to become part of a *Vicar
of Dibley* episode, which might be remembered
as my most famous partnership!

7

Finishing

SONG OF THE EARTH

Song of the Earth

JUNE, 2007

THE ROYAL BALLET, COVENT GARDEN, LONDON

Sir Kenneth MacMillan's *Song of the Earth*
premiered in 1965. I was very fortunate to have
Sir Kenneth there when I first learnt it in 1990. He
was instrumental in the early part of my career,
moving me from Sadler's Wells Royal Ballet to
The Royal Ballet and creating two works on
me, Princess Rose in *The Prince of the Pagodas*
and Masha in *Winter Dreams*. Very sadly, Sir
Kenneth died unexpectedly in 1992. He left an
extraordinary legacy to the ballet world. *Song*
made a deep and lasting impression on me but
I did not get to perform it again for another
17 years. I had decided that the 2006/7 Season
was going to be my last year at The Royal
Ballet Company. When I saw *Song of the Earth*
scheduled in the repertoire for the very end of
the Season, it was as if Kenneth had chosen my
last show for me.

Song of the Earth

JUNE, 2007

THE ROYAL BALLET, COVENT GARDEN, LONDON

This was the first role that took me to another level – it opened another chapter on the emotions in dance. It had a real spirituality. I was fortunate to have my Director, the wonderful Dame Monica Mason coaching me and sharing her invaluable knowledge of her many performances of *Song*. She has a deep understanding of Sir Kenneth MacMillan's work, and this passing on of knowledge is essential for the success of The Royal Ballet's famous repertoire. On the left I am pictured with Carlos Acosta who is dancing the role of Death.

Song of the Earth
JUNE, 2007
THE ROYAL BALLET, COVENT GARDEN, LONDON

Set to the score of Mahler's song cycle, *Song of the Earth* is based on 8th century poems of the T'ang dynasty. The audience does not need to know the poems as Sir Kenneth's choreographic genius portrays the story and the emotions perfectly. Kenneth accurately depicted the continual presence of death in the lives of the Man and the Woman. I enjoyed the unnatural process of never coming eye to eye with Carlos Acosta but knowing he was always there, either behind me or partnering me.

Song of the Earth

JUNE, 2007

THE ROYAL BALLET, COVENT GARDEN, LONDON

These photographs show the beautiful clean
shapes and lines that Kenneth created in the
last movement, even when he was portraying
the emotional pulls between the three main
characters. Opposite is Carlos Acosta dancing
the role of Death, Gary Avis as the Man, and I
am the Woman. Also special and unusual about
this work is that there are Principal opera singers
on stage with you, creating even more of an
atmosphere. I always felt it was such a privilege
to be dancing to such exquisite voices.

Song of the Earth

JUNE, 2007

THE ROYAL BALLET, COVENT GARDEN, LONDON

Gary Avis, as the Man, partnered me brilliantly
in the last song. Facing the inevitability of
separation through death, you have to create
the real sense of deep loss throughout the
climatic last pas de deux. You must keep this
energy and emotion flowing at all times, even in
moments of complete stillness. In this lift, I am
balancing on his shoulders and if Gary moved at
all I would fall.

Song of the Earth

JUNE, 2007

THE ROYAL BALLET, COVENT GARDEN, LONDON

I was so focused on trying to perfect every move of my last performance, that the feelings I had when I finished took me completely by surprise. I had always been proud that I had never lost my nerve or poise on stage during my career. But on this occasion I did a wonderful job of uncontrollably breaking down in tears when so many of my colleagues came on stage at the end, to be with me this last time. There were so many people there who meant so much to me: dance partners, coaches, Directors, the conductor and the Company itself. I was truly in shock. I couldn't have asked for a more poignant and appropriate end to my career. I felt truly blessed.

Chronology of Dèbuts in Major Roles with The Royal Ballet

All performances are at the Royal Opera House unless otherwise specified.

17 November 1988	Lilac Fairy in Petipa's *The Sleeping Beauty*
22 November 1988	Created Principal role in Bintley's *Spirit of Fugue*
31 December 1988	Winter Fairy in Ashton's *Cinderella*
14 March 1989	Soloist in Balanchine's *Capriccio (Rubies)*
17 March 1989	Lady May in Ashton's *Enigma Variations*
14 April 1989	Swan in Petipa and Ivanov's *Swan Lake*
18 May 1989	Second solo Shade in Petipa's *La Bayadère*
27 May 1989	Gamzatti in Petipa's *La Bayadère*
12 October 1989	Agnus Dei role in MacMillan's *Requiem*
7 December 1989	Created role of Princess Rose in MacMillan's *The Prince of the Pagodas*
26 January 1990	Lead female role in Chaboukiani's *Laurentia*
3 February 1990	Odette/Odile in Petipa and Ivanov's *Swan Lake*
21 April 1990	Myrtha in Perrot/Coralli/Petipa's *Giselle*
28 April 1990	*Pas de Deux* in Bintley's *Galanteries*
28 April 1990	*Pas de Deux* in Page's *Pursuit*
17 May 1990	White Woman in MacMillan's *Song of the Earth*
July 1990	Created female role in MacMillan's *Farewell Pas de Deux* at The London Palladium
26 October 1990	Bethena Waltz in MacMillan's *Elite Syncopations*
29 November 1990	Aria 1 Woman in Balanchine's *Stravinsky Violin Concerto*
29 November 1990	Created role in Brown's trio in Page's *Bloodlines*
1 December 1990	Raymonda in Petipa's *Raymonda*
26 December 1990	Sugar Plum Fairy in Ivanov's *The Nutcracker*
7 February 1991	Created role of Masha in MacMillan's *Winter Dreams*
10 April 1991	*Pas de Deux* in Balanchine's *Agon*
5 June 1991	Hostess in Nijinska's *Les Biches*
4 November 1991	Woman in Balanchine's *Tchaikovsky Pas de Deux*
20 November 1991	Lead roles in Tuckett's *Present Histories*
3 December 1991	Ballerina in the Second Movement of Balanchine's *Symphony in C*
13 February 1992	Principal woman in Forsythe's *In the middle, somewhat elevated*
17 February 1992	Principal woman in Ashton's *Trois Gymnopèdies/Monotones*
29 February 1992	Manon in MacMillan's *Manon*
17 May 1992	Nikiya in Petipa's *La Bayadère* Tokyo (then at The Royal Opera House 31 March 1997)
29 October 1992	Mitzi Caspar in MacMillan's *Mayerling*
4 January 1993	Cinderella in Ashton's *Cinderella*
12 January 1993	Terpischore in Balanchine's *Apollo*
30 January 1993	Princess Aurora in Petipa's *The Sleeping Beauty*
30 April 1993	*Pas de Trois* in Balanchine's *Ballet Imperial*
4 June 1993	The Prostitute in Tetley's *La Ronde*
4 June 1993	Black Queen in de Valois' *Checkmate*
5 June 1993	The Siren in Balanchine's *Prodigal Son*
30 October 1993	Juliet in MacMillan's *Romeo and Juliet*
24 November 1993	*Pas de Deux* in Forsythe's *Herman Schmerman*
15 December 1993	*Pas de Deux* in Balanchine's *Ballet Imperial*
6 April 1994	Princess Aurora in Dowell's *The Sleeping Beauty* premiere at The Kennedy Centre, Washington
9 December 1994	Principal woman in Ashton's *Raymonda pas de deux*
25 January 1995	Principal woman in Balanchine's *Duo Concertant* in Dance Bites tour (then at The Royal Opera House 6 April 1995)
20 May 1995	Giselle in Perrot/Coralli/Petipa's *Giselle* at Sejong (then at The Royal Opera House 26 July 1995)
9 December 1995	Created role of Truth on Toe in Tharp's *Mr Wordly Wise*

7 February 1996	Created role in Hart's *Dances with Death*
19 March 1996	Principal woman in Page's *...now languorous, now wild...* in Dance Bites tour
15 April 1996	Sacred love in Ashton's *Illuminations*
3 May 1996	Kschessinka in MacMillan's *Anastasia*
18 October 1996	Created Principal woman in Wheeldon's *Pavane pour une infanta dèfunte*
13 February 1997	Principal woman (Van Hamel) role in Tharp's *Push Comes to Shove*
30 April 1997	Created role in Tetley's *Amores*
12 February 1998	Nikiya in Petipa's *La Bayadère* at the Kirov (Mariinsky company), St Petersberg
25 February 1998	Nikiya in Makarova's *La Bayadère* at the Australian Ballet Company, Sydney
21 March 1998	Command Performance of International Ballet, Dallas, USA
15 June 1998	Black Queen in de Valois' *Checkmate,* 100th birthday, Ninette De Valois Celebration
15 June 1998	Beriosova solo in Ashton's *Birthday Offering* at The Barbican, London
19 June 1998	Fonteyn *Pas de Deux* in Ashton's *Birthday Offering* at The Barbican, London
12 June 1999	An evening with Darcey Bussell at the Edinburgh Festival Theatre
16 June 1999	An evening with Darcey Bussell at Hampton Court Palace
9 July 1999	Principal woman in Baldwin's *Towards Poetry*
23 July 1999	Principal woman in Balanchine's *Serenade*
23 November 1999	Principal woman in Martin's *Barber Violin Concerto, second movement*
8 December 1999	Principal woman in Neumeier's *Lento*, Celebration of International Choreography
4 February 2000	Principal woman in Balanchine's *Ballet Imperial*
29 February 2000	Principal woman in Ashton's *Les Rendezvous*
4 May 2000	Principal woman in Robbins' *The Concert*
27 June 2000	Principal woman in Wheeldon's *There Where She Loves*
28 October 2000	Principal woman in Corder's *Dance Variations*
26 January 2002	Principal woman in Baynes' *Beyond Bach*
20 May 2002	Principal woman in Wheeldon's *Tryst*
22 October 2002	Principal woman in Morris' *Gong*
8 March 2003	Aurora in Makarova's *The Sleeping Beauty*
July 2004	Aurora in Ashton's *Awakening pas de deux* at the Metropolitan Opera House, New York
4 November 2004	Sylvia in Ashton's *Sylvia*
2 June 2005	Natalya in Ashton's *A Month in the Country*
16 October 2005	The Bride in Howard's *Le Fête Étrange*
5 November 2005	Sylvia in *Act 3 pas de deux* at Buckingham Palace, London
December 2005	Principal woman in Marriot's *Tanglewood*
18 March 2006	The Woman in Roland Petit's *Le Jeune Homme et la Mort* at La Scala, Milan, Italy
5 June 2006	Air in Ashton's *Homage to the Queen*, in celebration of Her Majesty the Queen's 80th birthday
17 November 2006	Sanguinic in Balanchine's *The Four Temperaments*
19 March 2007	Principal woman in Balanchine's *Theme and Variations*
16 May 2007	Farewell shows at Sadler's Wells Theatre, London
8 June 2007	White Woman in MacMillan's *Song of the Earth*, Final Show

2002
LONDON

This was shot by Bryan Adams in his kitchen.
I had to balance in an arabesque wearing a hired
Marilyn Monroe dress. There were two ladders
on either side of me and assistants holding
pieces of fishing line attached to my dress.
This photo was based on a sculpture of a 1920s
dancer Bryan had seen.

2006
LONDON

For a collection titled British Muses, all shot
by Bryan Adams. I am in a stunning semi-
transparent dress by Alexander McQueen.
I needed platform stilettos to wear this
extraordinary dress because of its length, but
it wasn't easy to strike a still pose in them.

Photo Credits

2004
LONDON

In this commission for the Mandarin Oriental Hotel Group, we shot many dances poses trying to get a full variety of looks. We spent the day moving around the Opera House using every free space we could. The photo on the left captures me resting between turns. Being a truly generous and lovely person, Mary McCartney made the whole experience go very smoothly. At the end of the day we went outside for the last shot and it transpired that she can even make an alley way look theatrical.

FLETCHER SIBTHORP 2006

This is a charcoal painting of Christopher Wheeldon's ballet *DGV*. I first sat for a portrait for Fletcher at the age of 19 and he was just two years older than me. This is one of the many works that he has painted of me dancing and one of his beautiful paintings of me hangs in a studio at The Royal Ballet Lower School, White Lodge. Fletcher has an extraordinary ability to capture movement in his paintings and has painted many Principals in the world of ballet and flamenco.

ALLEN JONES 1997

I was thrilled to learn that the National Portrait Gallery had commissioned my portrait and that Allen Jones, being such a distinguished pop artist, wanted to paint it. I looked forward to working with an artist who was going to push the boundaries. Allen was divine, and a complete gentleman. He photographed me in many poses and was fascinated by the line created when being 'en pointe'. Over the month of sitting, I often came in after a full day of rehearsing and was too tired to stand up, so Allen kindly let me fall asleep in his chair while he worked on my portrait.

Acknowledgements

My sincere thanks to everyone involved with the making of this book. It has been a pleasure working with the professional team at Hardie Grant Books, led by Julie Pinkham, and I thank them so much for creating such a beautiful photographic book on dance. My special thanks to Managing Editor Gordana Trifunovic whose patience, attention to detail and sense of style have been integral to this book.

Tracey Gibson's skills were put severely to the test having to track down photos from the other side of the world and I thank her for her persistence and delightful manner. Janine Limberg, my very dear friend, came to my rescue yet again. Present at nearly every shoot I ever did, she sourced photos and quotes, remembered dates and names I had forgotten, and as always, provided unflinching support.

My thanks to my publishing agent Fran Moore, who used all her experience and skill to guide me seamlessly through all the administrative necessities.

Sir Anthony Dowell, my former Director, has been so kind to write such a generous Foreword. I would like to thank everyone who took the time to write a quote for this book, it means so much to me to have your words included.

My thanks to my family, my Mum and Dad for being an ongoing fan club and my husband Angus for always agreeing with me (!), and my two beautiful girls Phoebe and Zoe for being incredibly patient with their arty mum.

As I look at the finished document, it brings back memories of so many wonderful people I worked with during my career, and I thank them all for being part of my dancing life. I would like to mention a few in particular. Firstly, my two Directors Sir Anthony Dowell and Dame Monica Mason, and my wonderful coach Donald MacLeary, who coached me for every single one of my years at The Royal Ballet. Secondly, my partners: Jonathan Cope, Christopher Saunders, Irek Mukhamedov, Adam Cooper, Zoltan Solymosi, Igor Zelensky, Carlos Acosta, Gary Avis, Edward Watson, Damien Welch and Roberto Bolle. Lastly, the choreographers who created works on me: Sir Kenneth MacMillan, David Bintley, Ashley Page, Christopher Wheeldon, Glenn Tetley, Michael Corder, Mark Baldwin, Twyla Tharp, John Neumeier and Alastair Marriott.

For almost my entire career I was part of the exceptional Company that is The Royal Ballet. The talent assembled was quite unbelievable, from the choreographers, the back stage heroes, the musicians, fellow performers through to the Directors. The photographs you see in these pages are a tribute to them and to the opportunities that The Royal Ballet afforded me.

I would like to express my most heartfelt thanks to all the photographers whose work is featured in this book for their generosity and cooperation: Bryan Adams, Rudy Amisano, Holger Badekow, Marco Brescia, Andrew Cockrill, Bill Cooper, Anthony Crickmay, Jillian Edelstein, Arthur Elgort, Robbie Jack, Allen Jones, Paul Kolnik, Annie Leibovitz, Laurie Lewis, Mary McCartney, Jim McFarlane, Nigel Norrington, Johan Persson, Michael S. Radley, David Secombe, Fletcher Sibthorp, Lord Snowdon, Leslie E Spatt, Mario Testino, and Jimmy Wormser. I thank all the ballet photographers for their time and dedication to the art of ballet.

To all the photographers whose work is featured, I hope this book is worthy of your amazing skill, dedication and artistry.

2004

LONDON

One of the fabulous and outrageous photos taken for the World Gold Council. They were holding an International jewellery design competition and we needed to shoot 20 different pieces. It was a one-off week of extraordinary creativity with the wonderful John Swannell. We did four very different shoots all styled by Hilary Alexander.

Sylvia

MAY 2007

SADLER'S WELLS THEATRE, LONDON

On stage at the wings of Sadler's Wells Theatre
with the producers of my Farewell shows, my
old friends and colleagues, Michael Nunn and
Billy Trevitt.

Published in 2012 by Hardie Grant Books

Hardie Grant Books (Australia)
Ground Level, Building One
658 Church St
Richmond, Victoria 3181
www.hardiegrant.com.au

Hardie Grant Books (UK)
Dudley House, North Suite
34–35 Southampton Street
London WC2E 7HF
www.hardiegrant.co.uk

The moral rights of the author has been asserted.
Copyright text © Darcey Bussell 2012
Copyright photography, see pages 214–215

National Library of Australia Cataloguing-in-Publication Data:
Darcey Bussell / Darcey Bussell.
ISBN: 978 1 74270 352 7 (hbk.)
Special Edition 978 1 74270 469 2
Bussell, Darcey.
Ballerinas--Great Britain--Pictorial works.
Ballerinas--Great Britain--Biography.
Ballet dancers--Pictorial works.
Ballet--Great Britain--History.
Ballet--Great Britain--Pictorial works. 792.8028092

Managing Editor: Gordana Trifunovic
Design Manager: Heather Menzies
Designer: Stephen Smedley, Tonto Design
Picture researcher: Tracey Gibson
Production: Penny Sanderson
Colour reproduction by Splitting Image Colour Studio
Printed and bound in China by 1010 Printing International Limited

From page 2:

MARIO TESTINO DECEMBER 1999

—

Shot for the Millennium issue of Vogue. Mario
photographed an amazing compilation of famous
people, principally from the arts, in a basement
night-club. All these cool and 'it' people were
piling in and Mario wanted me to wear a tutu...
'Great!' I told him... 'only if I keep my jeans on!'
Photographed with the extraordinary Michael
Clark, contemporary choreographer.

From page 4:

ARTHUR ELGORT DECEMBER 1989

—

Aged 20, my first major fashion photo shoot
took a whole week in New York. Cynthia Harvey,
Principal dancer of ABT, and I were photographed
for an 8 page spread of dance fashion for
American Vogue. Arthur was charming and made
this slightly nerve-racking experience wonderful
and unforgettable.

I dedicate this book to my husband Angus Forbes, for his patience and love.

Left: Zoe Forbes in my tutus, in my dressing
room. Right: Phoebe Forbes and my coach
Donald MacLeary after a performance of *Giselle*.